I WANT TO BE HER!

HOW FRIENDS & STRANGERS
HELPED SHAPE MY STYLE

ANDREA LINETT
ILLUSTRATIONS BY ANNE JOHNSTON ALBERT

ABRAMS IMAGE, NEW YORK

FOR MOM AND DAD

Editors: Rebecca Kaplan and David Cashion
Designers: Michelle Ishay and Danielle Young
Cover Design: Gabriele Wilson
Production Manager: Ankur Ghosh

Library of Congress Cataloging-in-Publication Data:

Linett, Andrea.
  I want to be her! : how friends and strangers helped shape my
style / by Andrea Linett ; illustrated by Anne Johnston Albert.
    pages cm
  ISBN 978-1-4197-0401-7 (alk. paper)
1. Linett, Andrea. 2. Clothing and dress. 3. Beauty, Personal. I.
Title.
  TT507.L527 2012
  646'.3—dc23
                              2012008023

Printed and bound in China
10 9 8 7 6 5 4 3 2 1

Abrams Image books are available at special discounts when purchased in
quantity for premiums and promotions as well as fundraising or educational
use. Special editions can also be created to specification. For details, contact
specialsales@abramsbooks.com or the address below.

THE ART OF BOOKS SINCE 1949
115 West 18th Street
New York, NY 10011
www.abramsbooks.com

CONTENTS

INTRODUCTION

I'm not really sure when or why kids decide that they want to be something other than a cliché, like a model or fireman, to something more specific and real, like an advertising executive or a district attorney. I've always known that I needed to be in a field that was fast-paced and filled with glamour, fashion, and fun—otherwise, what was the point? After all, I grew up watching my mother, an advertising writer and creative director, in just such an environment, and she seemed to have a great time with her work every day. Practically from the time I was just out of onesies, I was styling myself (or dreaming of styling myself) in whatever was trendy at the time. But when my family moved from the groovy East Village to the more conservative Summit, New Jersey, suddenly all of my street inspiration disappeared. There was nothing much to look at in that town (save for some beautiful trees and pretty houses). Most of the kids just wore practical play clothes like Levi's and T-shirts. It was during this time that I became obsessed with fashion magazines like *Seventeen*, *Vogue*, and *Mademoiselle*, and books on style (especially the series by Francesco Scavullo). I spent hours poring over their glossy pages, fantasizing about being as effortlessly chic as the women in the pictures. I also loved music—I remember being beyond excited to bring in my parents' Bette Midler album, *The Divine Miss M*, to second grade show-and-tell. I instructed Miss Conway to put the needle on the first song on side A. As a super-sexed-up version of "Do You Want to Dance?" blared through the portable record player's single speaker, I noticed Miss Conway looking like she might pass out, and all of my classmates' eyes glazing over. It suddenly occurred to me that I would spend the next several years surrounded by people who just didn't get it.

When I was about twelve, I'd sit at home and make my

own version of Saks and Bloomingdale's catalogs, complete with all the copy and art ("A. Gold-tone initial earrings, $12.50 . . . B. Personalized cuff bracelet, $19.50 . . . "). For me inspiration was everywhere except for my immediate, everyday surroundings. It came from being in the chic designer boutiques, and Loehmann's back room with my mom, and from the great movies that my parents took me to—*Annie Hall*, *Manhattan*, *The Great Gatsby*, *All That Jazz*, *The Sting*—all of which showcased fashion and lifestyles in such a glamorous way.

I love good style, any kind of good style, and I get inspired by someone new every minute—a Dead Head, a rich Italian lady . . . I don't discriminate, as long as they put themselves together in a fabulous way. Whether their look is rock 'n' roll, preppy, or even a little tacky, each of these people knows who they are and how they want to look, and I eat it up. I am not above following a girl down the street like a crazed stalker, just to get a closer look at her face or shoes or necklace. I have no shame.

Long before style blogs, people simply checked out each other's look on the street. If you were lucky enough to, say, go to Paris or somewhere equally exotic style-wise, you could really come back with something special. I've always paid close attention to everyone around me, from as early as age five, when I would stare at the cool hairdressers where my mom got her haircut, all the way up through high school, when my best friend and I would hang out in New York City and East Hampton and take in all the glamour of the locals and off-duty models. College was like one big live fashion blog, with thousands of fashion-forward girls trolling the campus at any given time. Then, when I landed my first job at a fashion magazine and stayed on that track for many years, life was one big fashion inspiration (hey, for one thing, I got to see everything way before the public did!).

But people-watching is nothing new. We all do it (and I'm sure the Gibson girls, flappers, and bobby soxers all got inspiration from one another). That's what's so great about stoops and cafés: They allow you to sit for hours while checking out everyone who walks by. All you have to do is hang out downtown to spot cool chicks with wild hair and leather jackets and you're suddenly compelled to go home and change out of your sensible corduroys and rain boots to rock something sexier and more fun. And truthfully, if not prepared, a trip up to the doctor on Madison and 87th makes me feel like, well, frankly, a dirtbag. One look at all those perfectly coiffed women with their $12,000 handbags and chic sunglasses and I get all confused again. Such is fashion and style. If you truly love it, you can appreciate all of it. I consider myself a gourmand of fashion. And that's what makes it so much fun.

So, this book is really a love letter to anyone who has ever made me do a double-take and wish that I could be in her shoes, even if only for a minute.

—Andrea Linett

CHILDHOOD

or

*Grown-ups Get
All the Good Clothes*

Growing up, we lived in a two-bedroom apartment in a six-story brick building on East Eighth Street in New York, where I shared a room with my older sister, Dana. Looking back, it seems quite fitting that at the time, the entire strip of Eighth Street between Sixth Avenue and Broadway was lined with fabulous shoe store after fabulous shoe store. It was where I snagged my first pair of mini yellow Olaf Daughters clogs and, later, my coveted high-school cowboy boots. Back then we really didn't have much money to spend on clothes, but what we did have was an industrious mom with great style.

My first shopping memory is of my mother taking us down the street to Casual Kids, a no-frills clothing store that was basically one big stockroom. There were no attractive mannequins or clever marketing displays to inspire us in any way; to shop here, you had to have imagination. Every last piece of clothing was unapologetically housed in clear wrap and jammed onto overly crowded metal bars. There were no dressing rooms, and we had to change in between the plastic-lined racks. Dana and I would each get a couple of cute outfits a season, and then for everything else, Mom got creative. She invented my favorite look, which she dubbed "hot pants." This was basically a stylish euphemism for summer shorts with tights under them. But the idea alone was so alluring that in the morning when she yelled out, "Who wants to wear hot pants?" I knew it would be a good day. So what if I was in kindergarten? In my mind, hot pants gave me immediate far-out status!

When I was four or five years old, right before we moved out of the city, I remember my mother picking me up at a neighbor's house at the exact moment when the opening credits of a new show came on TV. There were animated partridge birds hatching out of their shells and walking across the screen to the lyrics "Hello world, here's a song that we're singin'; Come on, get happy!" Then Susan Dey or the sublime and foxy David Cassidy must have walked into frame in bell-bottomed jeans, a zip-front ribbed T-shirt, and puka shells, because I was transfixed. Mom literally had to drag me away from the set, my little mouth agape. I couldn't believe the insane grooviness right before my eyes: a whole world of cool teenagers with long, silky hair and good singing voices. I always had short hair. (My mom was busy—she took my sister and me to the barber for practical pixie cuts. You wouldn't find any No More Tangles in our house.) So naturally I became obsessed with hip teenage girls with straight, shiny, parted-in-the-middle, super-long hair.

TV was my number-one source of inspiration, and soon, of course, came the amazing Brady Bunch. I couldn't care less about Cindy and her cartoonish pigtails, but Jan and Marcia— in all their golden, long-haired glory, always wearing cute minidresses with mod Mary Janes and going on dates in eternally sunshine-filled Southern California—now *they* were awesome. I couldn't wait to be their age and was forever trying to figure out how to get the family to relocate to Hollywood, since I was convinced that that was where all the action was. If only we lived there, Dana and I could easily be on TV or get a singing contract like the Bradys or the Partridges—not to mention being able to walk around a beautiful, sunny high-school campus, notebooks pressed to our geometric-print-clad chests, smiling and waving to potential boyfriends between classes. *Sigh.*

Other glamorous fixtures in our childhood were Mom's brothers Bob and Gerson. They were young and handsome. Mom has always liked to assign everyone a celebrity doppel-gänger, so Bob was "a real Robert Redford type," while Gerson looked more like Dustin Hoffman. Bob was a divorced real estate lawyer/developer who seemed to live a movie-star-glamorous life. He would go to Martinique and bring back a cool Club Med–emblazoned burlap beach bag, or Paris and bestow upon me some tiny little perfume bottle that, looking back, was probably picked up at Charles de Gaulle, but who cared! That little vial of Infini de Caron in its sexy '70s-modern bottle was a shining star on my otherwise messy, cluttered bureau. I would tell any friend who would listen that it was real *perfume*, not cologne, that my uncle brought back from Paris, and it cost TWENTY DOLLARS! Not wanting to waste it or ever use it up, I would only occasion-ally allow myself the teeniest dab. It smelled like what I assumed all the models in the fashion spreads, with their crimped hair, smoky eyes, and dark, glossy burgundy lips, smelled like.

Once Uncle Bob took me to Serendipity on East Sixtieth Street for frozen hot chocolate and let me pick out T-shirts from their gift shop for Dana and me. They had that great French cut with a perfect scoop neck and little cap sleeves, and mine said "Sur la Plage" on it. Hers had a giant Andy Warhol–esque draw-ing of a Coca-Cola bottle cap. Pure New York City glamour!

We moved out of the city in 1971, and I spent most of grade school not fitting in. Even though there was pretty much no

+ = hotpants!

Perfume from Paris

infini
CARON

Sur la Plage

pure glamour!

visual stimulation at Wilson Elementary, my fashion obsession kept growing stronger, and in sixth grade I insisted on dressing up in the latest runway look: a Black Watch plaid skirt suit with a matching tie-neck white blouse. Why I thought an eleven-and-a-half-year-old needed a sensible business suit, and why my mom agreed to get me one (and lastly, why they even made them for kids) remain mysteries. But there I was in the sixth-grade class picture, with a puffy Dorothy Hamill haircut, braces, and brown leather Earth Shoes, showing off my power-woman office look.

I couldn't wait for the weekends. Saturday mornings were always filled with excitement because that's when *American Bandstand* came on. This show was the 1970s version of a fashion magazine come to life set to good songs you could dance to. I would anxiously await the theme song, "Bandstand Boogie" by Barry Manilow—"We're goin' hoppin' (hop), we're goin' hoppin' today; where things are poppin' (pop), the Philadelphia way; we're gonna drop in (drop), on all the music they play, on the Bandstand BANDSTAND!"—and sit glued to the set looking for pretty girls with cool haircuts and fun outfits dancing for the camera. When I saw a pair of giant wide-leg Landlubber overalls with big orange buttons, I went into a frenzy and decided I needed them immediately. Sitting on the red shag carpet in my parents' room, I fashioned my own suspenders out of old jeans. Of course, this hand-sewn mess of a creation was strictly for lip-synching in the mirror of my bedroom. I also loved Mary Tyler Moore and her cool

Jewish friend, Rhoda, with their seemingly fun, freewheeling single lives. When Rhoda got her own show and moved to New York City, all I wanted to do was check out her outfits— she was very 1940s-meets-Studio-54, and I loved it. One of my favorite songs at the time was Odyssey's "Native New Yorker." I longed to be like the girl they sang about, "riding the subways, running with people up in Harlem, down on Broadway," preferably sporting a satin jumpsuit, gold disco bag, and heels—I too could be "the heart and soul of New York City"!

The kids at school didn't experiment with anything more daring than Levi's and maybe the odd poncho here and there. They dressed their age and didn't care. I, however, was ready to look like my mom and all the other cool older chicks I came into contact with. The only problem was, I was a tiny kid and everything was made for teenagers and women. I did, however, find an amazing stretchy, burgundy bell-bottomed leisure suit at Bloomingdale's (think Osmonds stage wear) that made me feel like I had really made it to the big time. Never mind my puffy in-between-length nothing hairstyle and buck teeth— I felt like a badass. When buffalo platform sandals were all the rage (my mom had a pair that must have been about five inches high), I wanted them. I *needed* them. But of course the kid versions were all low wedges, so alas, I had to settle. A few years ago, I was walking down lower Fifth Avenue with my then nine-year-old niece, Libby, and as we passed Aldo, she gazed longingly at a pair of studded sandals in the window and

Tootsie Roll
Lipsmackers

my first suit

Mom's
sandals

proclaimed, "All the good stuff only comes in grown-up sizes!" Now she's thirteen and wants clothes from the juniors department, which she figures she can alter. I totally get it.

If my mom didn't want to buy me a desperately desired article of clothing, there was always her dad, Grandpa Jack. He was constantly playing poker or hitting the OTB, and he usually spent his winnings on us. Sometimes, if we were really lucky, he would take us shopping in the city. It was on one of these trips that I procured my had-to-have-them-or-I'd-surely-die clear fisherman jelly sandals that I must have seen in a magazine (or on some chic woman in Manhattan). I also begged him for Jordache jeans. Who could resist that commercial featuring the hot city girl with long, bouncy blond hair, working (modeling around on a white seamless) and playing (bopping around bars and dancing with a cute guy) day and night? When I told Grandpa Jack the price, he simply said, "No way," so I settled for skintight, faded-baby-blue "French" jeans from the discount store. They might not transform me from an awkward tween into that sophisticated model in the commercial, but they were a fine substitute.

Aside from my favorite plaid skirt suit, sixth grade also brought my sartorial match, my new friend Kathy, whom I first encountered in Sunday school. (I knew she was cool when she invited me over and threw a David Bowie record on the turntable: "Ch-ch-ch-ch-changes!" We must have listened to that song a thousand times.) We both loved fashion, and

Kathy had a very private, sitcom-worthy attic bedroom, complete with its own bathroom. Perhaps the most enviable thing about Kathy was her skin-care regimen, which involved some kind of fancy, delicious-smelling almond-and-honey scrub (I still use one because of her—I like Mario Badescu's, if anyone cares). It all felt very grown-up and aspirational to me, since my room abutted my sister's and the most glamorous product I had used thus far was that clear-orange Neutrogena face soap from the drugstore.

Kathy and I became inseparable and wore all of the same things (if people were going to make fun of us, we needed support). In seventh grade we made a pact to go back to school in style—no more pussyfooting around! *Seventeen*'s September issue was showing the latest footwear and we agreed, hands down, that the choice for our successful foray into teenage life had to be Bass saddle shoes. After much deliberation, Kathy picked the classic tan color, and I went for the more unusual gray. We bravely showed up at school and were met with lots of snickers and finger-pointing, but we held our heads high—we knew what was what.

Another trend from our fashion bible that we couldn't pass up: little 1940s-style dresses worn with heels and ankle socks. Even though this look was strictly for editorial spreads and cool city women, Kathy went for it anyway. There she was, strolling down the halls of Summit Junior High in her little frock and sexy shoes. I was a little jealous of her courageous attitude, and while I did get my own puff-sleeved, multicolored, heart-print dress with a skinny patent-leather belt, I can't remember if I actually went through with the whole ankle-socks-and-Candie's part myself.

There were so many things for me and Kathy to be obsessed about. Like that 1978 Nair ad in *Seventeen*—a glorious full-page bleed depicting four girls in the most incredible satin tank/gym shorts suits and roller skates doing a cancan kick. Kathy and I lost it. How in God's name could we get our dorky little hands on these stunning little suits?! I wanted a baby-blue one. My mom's answer was a flat-out no, because really, where would I ever wear it? Kathy's mom said no too. Then when we went to the junior-high dance, we were dying of jealousy over Pam Long's black satin jacket/pant combo as she showed off her moves in the dance that went with the eponymous song "Le Freak." We were also enamored of Brooke Shields's look in *Pretty Baby*, which, come to think of it, we never even saw (if we had, we surely would have been grossed-out by the subject matter). The posters were enough to get us going—our idol looking all gorgeous in a white cotton nightgown with that enviable curled hair. We needed to look exactly like her, so off we went, to the local hair salon for perms. I was so protective of mine that every time I dunked my head in the lake at camp that summer, I'd quickly bob back up and squeeze the excess moisture from my curls, lest the nasty lake water pull them loose. I barely combed my hair either (for the same reason) and ended up with a rat's nest on my head. Not very Brookeish in the end.

Kathy and I wasted a lot of hours calling boys who didn't necessarily want us to, and sitting in her room listening to albums while trying to inhale Marlboro Lights without coughing. Around this time, Kathy convinced me that my long hair was getting me nowhere. I was emulating my favorite teen models like Brooke and Lisanne, and they *never* had feathered-back hair. It just wasn't *fashion*, and I wanted to live in a high-style magazine fantasy land. That kind of hair was for the real world—and sitcoms like *Three's Company* and *One Day at a Time*. (I never understood why Mackenzie Phillips wanted that Captain and Tennille hairdo when she could just grow it out and look like her sexy on-screen sister Barbara.) But Kathy finally got me to cut my hair so that with just a little help from a curling iron, it would flip back. I also started wearing Maybelline blush instead of pinching my cheeks for color. And miraculously it worked. One night we went to an all-night Jewish Community Center party that they called a "vigil" to make it sound cool. It started at the Livingston roller rink, where I skated around in my skintight baby-blue French jeans—the label said *Jean St. Tropez*, but now that I think of it, they were probably made in China—with a giant "Good & Plenty" comb sticking out of my back pocket that looked like an actual flat box of the candy. A cute older boy started flirting with me right away and Kathy gave me a big "I told you so" grin.

My awesome comb!

'40s dress

Candies

CARYL

As far back as I can remember, my mom was always the epitome of style and taste. Many women I know recall their mothers putting on lipstick and doing their hair to get ready for a party, but my memories are a little different. My mom was no typical suburban housewife prettying herself up for the bridge get-together. She was a hip working woman with a cool job as an advertising creative director; she would come to my school on career day and explain the details of her professional life while I wriggled in my little seat, beaming with pride. My mom wasn't at home baking cookies or carpooling us to school—she was out in the real world, making money and looking glamorous! She had dark, almost-black, shiny hair that went from super pixie-short in the early '60s (when she wore round wire-rimmed John Lennon shades) to a groovy shag to a page-boy cut in the '70s. Mom usually sported a big Georg Jensen silver pendant and bracelets that my dad bought her, and a classic gold Cartier tank watch, but she was never into conventional diamonds or anything. Her clothes were the prefect mix of American and European chic and included tweed skirt suits with sexy knee-high boots, but she also mixed it up with funkier stuff, like a crazy baby-blue denim suit with sequins on the back in the shape of a bucking rodeo cowboy.

Whenever Mom was filming a commercial, she let us take the day off from school to come and watch, figuring it was educational. And when school was closed for a holiday, I would go to her office, which was like playing grown-up in the best possible way. We would arrive at the ad agency and Mom, in some cool outfit like an Annie Hall–inspired herringbone blazer, pleated pants, and high burgundy boots, would settle into her office, grab a cup of coffee in a Styro-foam cup, and take me around, intro-ducing me to art directors, account executives, secretaries, and ad traffickers. I would anxiously await the food truck that would pull up in the parking lot at around 9:30. While all the ladies paid for their cottage cheese and fruit, I'd grab a delicious donut and some chocolate milk. Mom would always give me a creative assignment and I would sit in an empty office, working on the latest campaign. I marveled at what I perceived to be everyone's easy, breezy day, and couldn't wait to be free from the confines of school and go to work like these lucky ducks.

FRANCINE

Since my mom worked pretty much full-time, we always had an array of babysitters. My least favorite was one whose name I can't remember. She actually used the fact that my sister and I were scared of Pinocchio to tease us. She once told Dana that she suddenly developed an inexplicable green dot on her nose, which of course terrified the poor six-year-old. My favorite babysitter was Francine, because she was French and pretty and cool. She had long, straight, shiny brown hair almost to her lower back, a cute son around my age named Jacques, and an MG convertible. I visited their loft once and Jacques's room was created with three panels of drywall and had no door. I just thought that was the most bohemian thing I had ever seen—who knows what bohemian means to a four-year-old, but I could just tell it wasn't normal, and that was good enough for me. Francine's husband once asked my dad for legal help because he thought she was cheating on him. My dad was a tax lawyer, so that never worked out.

* Take care of your skin
and hair, and you've got
two great accessories!

AMY/ELIZABETH

In 1969, my parents' best friends' daughter Amy was only about eight or nine years old, but she seemed like a teenager to me. She was a tall kid with long, dirty-blond hair and bangs who took ballet and reminded me of a Chrissy doll (the one whose hair grew with the push of a button on her back—if only *that* were possible). We lived in the same building, and I remember her hanging around after practice in a leotard and tights like a real ballerina would wear. She also had a retainer that made her talk funny, so I adopted that look and the accompanying lisp by bending a paper clip over my top teeth. I would follow her around and soak in her awesomeness whenever I could.

   Then suddenly something awful happened. Amy's family up and moved to Short Hills, New Jersey. There, she had a canopy bed with a Bobby Sherman poster over it. I would count the days when we could visit her in her big suburban house with a massive staircase (I always wanted a staircase for dramatic entrances and exits). When our family went to visit Amy's, I usually hung out with her younger brother David, making prank phone calls (my specialty) until their dad ripped the phone out of the wall. Sometimes, though, Amy and my sister let me hang out with them in Amy's teenage-fantasy room. She was always the first to get anything cool, and when Queen's "Bohemian Rhapsody" came out—and that was really something to hear—she had this amazing radio/eight-track cassette player with multi-colored disco lights that flashed to the beat. We listened to that crazy song over and over, marveling at how we'd never heard anything quite like it. We also loved Blue Suede's version of "Hooked on a Feeling" and loved watching the radio's lights pop around during the "Ooga chaka ooga ooga ooga chaka" part. When I was twelve and Amy was sixteen, I stayed with her family in East Hampton for a whole month and followed her every move. I tagged along to the all-ages night at the local club, and tailed her to the beach on our bikes. She always slept late in the mornings while I sat around wide-awake, bored out of my mind, excited to start the day. So of course I did what anyone in my position would do—I read her diary. When I got to the page that said, in her teenage cursive, "I wish Andrea wouldn't come to the beach with me. She's cramping my style. I'll never meet a guy," my heart sank. Her real name is Elizabeth and that's what she decided to go by in her adult life, but I still call her Amy.

ANY HAIRDRESSER AT PAUL MCGREGOR

I was five or six when my parents moved us from downtown New York City to Summit, New Jersey—possibly the preppiest of all Jersey towns, right after Princeton. Mom, with her shag haircut, bell-bottoms, and platforms, and Dad, with his mutton-chop sideburns and army-man bag, clearly did not choose our new hometown based on sartorial compatibility or political views. They had just heard that the schools were good and that it was a nice place for us to "play outside and ride bikes," and that was that. My mom still came into the city regularly to see friends, have lunch, go to the movies, and—most exciting for me—get her shag trimmed at Paul McGregor's salon. He was the man who had created Jane Fonda's look in *Klute*, so it was all very glamorous. The salon, a second-floor space on St. Mark's Place in the then truly grimy East Village, was housed in the future home of Boy Bar and Coney Island High. It had a creaky stairwell splattered with graffiti that scared me a little until my mom assured me (and I still think she was lying), "Oh, that's just decoration—it's all part of the experience!"

Once inside, while Mom had her layers refreshed, I would sit on the floor and stare at all the salon girls as they cut hair while swaying to songs like "Rock the Boat" and "Billy Don't Be a Hero." I can still see their perfect, tight, cap-sleeved, scoop-neck tees; groovy bell-bottoms; clear plastic belts; and platform sandals—all of which, in mini child-friendly versions, made it into my first-grade closet.

STEPHANIE

When I was eight, my parents sent my sister
and me to sleepaway camp. I started at the
babyish Lake Como (where I received a special
made-up dorky award for Most Cooperative
Camper) and moved up to the cooler older
camp, Nah-Jee Wah. This is where I met Stephanie, a pretty blue-eyed girl with short, shiny,
perfectly feathered-back brown hair. The camp
look was very specific and started with a pair
of faded overalls—always Lee, and always fitted (even better if they were a little short in the
crotch so the bib would hang low, about mid-
chest). Then there were the clogs; they had to be
suede and either navy or brown. I'll never forget
the sound of the wooden soles crunching along
the gravelly dirt camp roads as we walked to the
mess hall or ham-radio class. And the cool older
girls would wear silver nameplate necklaces (in
Hebrew, or block-lettered English), and they
always had two perfect white tan lines beaming
out of the top of their stretchy striped tube tops,
like those spotlights in Hollywood that serve as
navigational markers for fabulous star-studded
events. The coolest combination was the tube

✳ Sometimes a teeny dash
of bad taste can be sexy
in the mix.

top under the overalls, because it somehow sug-
gested more skin than if it wasn't covered up at
all. (I later wore this look to death with a tank
top instead of a tube during the Dexy's Mid-
night Runners "Come On Eileen" craze, but stay
with me . . .)

After camp ended, I would often go and
hang out at Stephanie's house in Union, New
Jersey, which was way different from my coun-
try-club-lovin' town. The girls there were tough.
They had sexy feathered hair, wore skintight
jeans, and smoked. Stephanie always piled on
tons of jewelry—all in fourteen-carat gold. If
one thing made me crazy with envy, it was her
charm holder on a long, shiny snake chain, jam-
packed with tiny versions of everything from a
Coke bottle to a blow dryer. I bought my own
at the Union Marketplace (one of the first flea
markets I'd ever experienced), but all I could
afford with my allowance was silver, so I had to
make do. One birthday—I was turning maybe
thirteen—my dad took me to the S. Marsh and
Sons jewelry store in Millburn, New Jersey, to
pick out my present. I thought of Stephanie
and chose a small, gold heart-shaped lock,
complete with a keyhole, on a short "S" chain.

I'll never forget her best friend, Risa, with amazing blond, feathered-back hair, eyeing my new necklace and proclaiming how cool it was that it sat perfectly in the little groove in my clavicle. Stephanie always did her short nails with dark-brown polish (which to me was kind of dirty and very grown-up and sexy at the same time), and her eyelashes were never without several coats of black Maybelline Great Lash mascara. In the winter she wore a little waist-length rabbit-fur jacket and shearling Candie's clogs. I basically went to her house to play dress-up and walk around the streets of Union like that until I had to go home.

LISANNE

It must have been all those weekends spent shopping with my mom at chic designer boutiques, because at around age ten, I became obsessed with fashion magazines and style books. I especially loved *Scavullo Women* and *Scavullo on Beauty*, by famed fashion photographer Francesco Scavullo. (I read them over and over again until I knew every picture and word by heart; I'm sure my parents would have been thrilled had I spent half as much time with my schoolbooks.) I also somehow acquired *Designing Your Face* by Way Bandy, *the* makeup artist of the time, whose method required a million tiny bottles of makeup and pencils and brushes and colors that were all laid out in chicly composed still lifes. Just reading it made me feel like I was part of the coolest club in the world (now I knew what contour was!), even though the only makeup I had ever tried was Maybelline powder blush and a big fat tube of Lip Smackers. (Tootsie Roll was the best because it not only smelled exactly like the candy, but it gave a little brown tint too.) Reading all these books and magazines made me realize that modeling was probably the most unconventional and amazing career a girl could have, And then came the holy grail: *Lisanne: A Young Model*, by Betsy Cameron. This book allowed me to follow the title heroine throughout her days at school and work. I dreamed of looking like she did in a pair of Levi's cords and a cable-knit crew neck, but I was also mesmerized by her wavy hair, which was long long long and the color of glistening sand. Lisanne also had the most glamorous life imaginable—one minute horsing around with classmates in science lab or practicing the flute, the next minute getting pinned and primped in a New York City photo studio to shoot some fabulous ad for electric-blue kids' overalls.

✳ Pieces like perfectly fitting corduroy jeans and classic Shetland sweaters still look great now.

BROOKE S.

When I first noticed her, she had the face of a beautiful grown woman, but she was my age (about ten). Without makeup, she looked like a gorgeous—and I mean *gorgeous*—kid. With makeup and professional *Vogue*-like styling, little Brooke was transformed into something otherworldly. She was just a child in the first Scavullo book; he and his team of glamour pros transformed her from a pretty young girl into a full-on sexy man-killer. (Turned out this was quite controversial and people questioned her mother's actions—"What kind of woman could let her own child pose like this?!"—but what did I know? I couldn't get enough.) Of course I asked my parents to buy me *The Brooke Book*, which was like her very own scrapbook filled with photos of her on and off duty (sometimes posing aside her regular old plain-Jane friends). My obsession continued on through *Blue Lagoon*. So what if she gave birth to her own brother's baby? She was so tan! She had those crazy long legs! And that hair! Then, when nothing came between her and her Calvins, I was all over it. Those pockets and that back pocket label were amazing. Too bad they looked really bad on me.

✳ Years later, few things look as effortlessly glamorous as a great-fitting pair of jeans and a silk blouse. With high heeled boots, this is still my go-to sort-of dressy look.

TRINI

When I was a kid, I loved any movie that starred good-looking kids; especially if it featured a pretty girl playing a good part, I was there—like *A Little Romance* with Diane Lane. (When she was on the cover of my parents' *Time* magazine instead of Henry Kissinger or someone equally boring, I greedily snatched it out of the mailbox before anyone got home from work.) One movie, *Rich Kids*, was about two friends, a boy and a girl around my age; they lived in big apartments in New York City with wealthy parents who basically ignored them, which frankly sounded like a little bit of heaven to me. They walked all over Manhattan in their cool outfits, pontificating about life like miniature Woody Allen characters. Trini Alvarado played Franny Phillips and embodied everything I wanted to be. She was a street-smart, sophisticated city kid with super-long hair that she wore in a single braid. If I remember correctly, she strolled the city wearing a perfect whiskey-colored suede fringe jacket, cream jeans,

a beaded Indian belt with a silver cowboy buckle, and cowboy boots. I immediately began my search for the belt and boots.

I didn't find the boots until much later—they were by Acme and were just the right sand suede. The jacket was too ambitious—I never would have gotten away with it, but I sure did dream. I'm actually still looking for it, now that I don't really care what other "kids" think.

✳ You can't go wrong with American classics. Worn together the right way, they scream "I've got style!" If a fringe jacket is too out-there for you, try a plain suede one in that perfect whiskey or deep brown.

HIGH SCHOOL

or

When Will I Be Free?

Just as I was entering freshman year, Kathy's parents started sending her to private school, and I had to enter high school best-friendless. Luckily, I met Anne J., and we became inseparable. This was right when music started to change. And of course, just as important as the new-wave sound were the cool new clothes that

The Go-Go's

Victorian blouse/
Sweatshirt Combo

Dangling Metaphor pants

went along with it. You could almost see the slick new-wave outfits, complete with black-and-white checks and pointy shoes, coming through the speakers. I played the Clash's debut album over and over again on my new basic stereo. The Cars song "Just What I Needed" was already a hit. (One boring afternoon, my sister sent me to the store to buy the 45, along with Prince's "I Wanna Be Your Lover," which we played until we couldn't listen anymore.) Then came the insanity that was the B-52s, with their exaggerated cartoon bouffant hairdos and almost scary robotic voices. (We loved them, but we didn't want to *be* them.) And then there were the Go-Gos, perhaps the most sartorially influential of them all. Belinda Carlisle made us crazy with excitement with her beaded '50s thrift-store dresses, pointy flats, and ironic, kooky cocktail-party jewelry. She was a fun, punky California girl, splashing around a public fountain with her good-time bandmates. Anne J. and I wanted to be just like them. Most of the "popular" girls still wore Fair Isle sweaters and Dickies, but what did we care? We wanted something bigger. Which isn't to say I hadn't ever tried to fit in by layering a cable-knit sweater over a boy's Oxford shirt over an Izod over a heart-printed turtleneck—this was just another one of my many fashion incarnations, not a way of life, like it was for everyone else.

Anne J. and I spent our time poring over magazines, spending weekends with my family at our place in East

Hampton, and taking the train into the city for window-shopping excursions. Sometimes we'd get off at Ninth Street, hitting the Village for good vintage and surplus finds. Our favorite stores were Flip on West Eighth Street and Unique Clothing Warehouse and Antique Boutique on lower Broadway. Sometimes we'd go directly to Midtown and dream-shop at Fiorucci, where we could maybe afford a poster or a tin canister. Another regular stop of ours was Il Makiage on East Fifty-first Street. This was a tiny makeup boutique at a time when most of the good stuff was really only sold in department stores. It felt very insider-y, like a place only for professional makeup artists and models. We fell in love with a lipstick they had there called Birthday Suit, which we slathered on like it was ChapStick. We now realize that Birthday Suit was basically a God-awful shade of beige that looked like Dermablend concealer smeared on our lips.

Back then, aside from Bloomingdale's, and occasionally Saks, my mom took us to discount places like Annie Sez and Hit or Miss, where I would find cool, and sometimes strange, things like my favorite pair of Girbaud jeans with writing on the hem and a hot pink striped cotton Cathy Hardwick sweater. Forget that they rarely had my size. I was small, but I would buy anything, sometimes even snagging size 8 pants and then just cinching them until they fit. At this point, our regular jeans and pants didn't look punky enough. Luckily

favorite shops

Birthday Suit
lipstick

before   after

Anne had a sewing machine, and she spent hours pegging every pair of pants we owned. Anne and I shared everything, mostly a pair of big green army harem pants (the kind that hung low at the crotch) lined in red flannel. These pants gave us an edge. We referred to them as our dangling metaphor pants and wore them into the ground.

While we loved the Clash, the Pretenders, Bow Wow Wow, the B-52s, and one-hit wonders like Haircut 100 and Men Without Hats, at one point, for no apparent reason, we became obsessed with the more traditional rock of Tom Petty. We would sit in the den watching MTV for hours until a Tom video came on. I finally scored tickets to see Tom Petty and the Heartbreakers at Brendan Byrne Arena, but no matter how much we begged, Anne's mom wouldn't let her go, so I ended up asking my friend Margaret. To prepare, I needed to do two things. First I figured I had to get some flowers together for Tom—good thing I was working as a flower salesgirl at the Union Market on Sundays. I grabbed whatever they let me, which was a bunch of uncool carnations, but he wouldn't care! Then I had to borrow Kathy's suede slouch boots (after all, Tom wore similar ones all the time). So what if Kathy's feet were about two sizes bigger than mine? That's what thick socks were for. So on the night of the show, I put on no fewer than two pairs of tube socks and the boots and wrote a note to Tom—*Hi Tom. My friend Anne's mom wouldn't let her come to the show. Here's her phone number...* —and tied it to the flowers. We got to the stadium and took our seats (which were pretty good, by the way, on the floor, maybe twenty rows back). I waited in anticipation until the right song—"Here Comes My Girl"—came on and I started heading up to the stage. It all felt like slow motion, me and my slouch boots sauntering closer and closer to Tom, until—WHAM! I threw the flowers at him. Imagine my excitement when they hit a startled Tom as he wailed on his guitar. Of course a giant security guard chased me back to my seat, but it was worth that slight embarrassment to be forever connected to Tom. After a couple of days, the excitement wore off as Anne and I realized he wasn't going to call. Maybe the note got lost in the fray? Anyway, a couple of months later we saw a photo in a music magazine of Tom on the stage getting hit by MY FLOWERS. He actually looked a little scared.

ANNE J.

Anne J. is my oldest friend. The first thing I noticed about
her was that she was super pretty and had really thick eye-
brows—just like Mariel Hemingway, but with darker hair.
The problem was that she was wearing a red monogrammed
"AMJ" crew-neck sweater, boring jeans, and blue suede clogs.
I saw a blank canvas, ripe for a makeover, and immediately
started talking to her. I shared some styling secrets with her,
like the fact that a kelly-green Izod (which I thought I was
wearing in an ironic, new-wave kind of way) really showed off
a tan, and I invited her to the most fun and glamorous place
on Earth: the Hamptons. I couldn't wait to make her look as
cool as she deserved to be. I told her she should wear edgier
stuff and get into modeling, so she chopped off her hair just
like our favorite model, Esmé Marshall, and borrowed my
denim jumpsuit, a find from Annie Sez. Somehow (this was
pre-Internet) I was able to find out when the modeling agencies were holding cattle calls (I even found out that that's
what casting calls were called in the industry) in the city.
Anne attended one and got signed with Ford—FORD!—right
away, and I got to live vicariously through her glamorous lifestyle. Ford held a party at Studio 54 to showcase their newest
girls, and Anne's face was projected onto the wall; when she
told me this, it was all I could talk about for a whole year and
then some (hey, look at me—I'm *still* talking about it!).

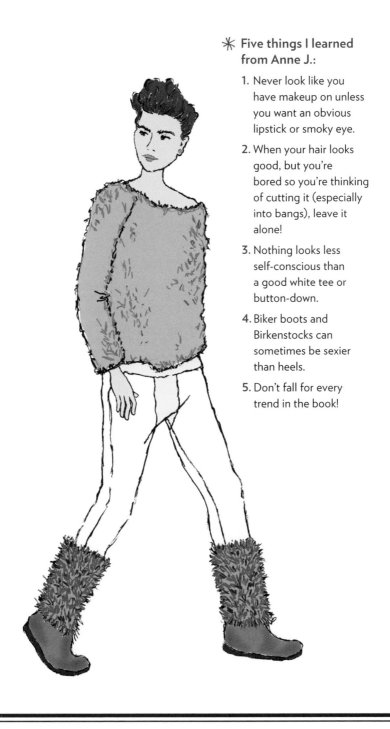

* **Five things I learned from Anne J.:**

1. Never look like you have makeup on unless you want an obvious lipstick or smoky eye.

2. When your hair looks good, but you're bored so you're thinking of cutting it (especially into bangs), leave it alone!

3. Nothing looks less self-conscious than a good white tee or button-down.

4. Biker boots and Birkenstocks can sometimes be sexier than heels.

5. Don't fall for every trend in the book!

We did everything together, enjoying many (mis)adventures at home and in the Hamptons. We loved devouring fashion magazines and conducting faux photo shoots. And even though I was five foot three and Anne a cool five nine, we shared clothes. The ones I remember best are the aforementioned "dangling metaphor" pants, and a handmade orange sweater that one of us wore to a drunken beach party and unknowingly filled with sand, and that later one of us lost on a trip. We still miss it. I also remember a beat-up straw hat with a little hole in it; a faded, stretched-out sweatshirt with the neck cut off; and a short, tiered chambray skirt. We took turns wearing that outfit to Snuggler's Cove, our favorite dive bar in Amagansett, for a little underage drinking.

After a lot of back and forth, Anne and I decided it would be fun to go to the prom—if for no other reason than to buy cute new outfits. First we secured our dates—hers was my cousin Brad (who is now married to a lovely husband) and mine was a cute blond guy from the next town over, a WASP whose dad founded the black hair-care salon Soul Scissors.

Anne and I were obsessed with whatever was on the pages of *Mademoiselle*, and the look in 1982 was white-cotton-Victorian-meets-modern-day-urban (think a gray sweatshirt over a high-neck cotton blouse with dangly pearl earrings and wispy hair) and Perry Ellis jackets with exaggerated puff sleeves. Anne found the perfect Laura Ashley cotton skirt suit on sale (it looked just like Perry Ellis!) and some cute flats; I got a high-neck nightgownlike dress that I deemed too short, so I compensated with a longer cotton slip underneath. I added white lace tights and black patent-leather wedge pumps. Having recently gone through a rock-star-wannabe phase, I had cut my hair into a Chrissie Hynde–Rod Stewart shag, complete with little rooster spikes on top. It was quite a statement, but tonight I wanted to look feminine, so I simply curled my hair and faked a pulled-back barrette look. (I later realized my dress resembled one of those turn-of-the-century white sauna machines with my little head popping out; if I had never looked at the pictures again, I might have had a great sartorial memory.)

When I went to college in Boston, Anne was off to Milan and other chic modeling locations like the Seychelles and Paris. When she came home for Christmas break in 1984, we listened to the latest Rolling Stones album, *Undercover*, as I sat in awe of her exotic Milanese style: fur-and-leather boots, a fuzzy stuffed-animal-like sweatshirt, and real gold-and-diamond jewelry that her thirty-five-year-old Italian playboy boyfriend had bought her.

I think my favorite Anne story is the time she went shopping in some avant-garde boutiques while on a shoot in Berlin. She tried on a tube skirt, emerged from the dressing room, and asked the salesgirl why it was so tight: "Is it one size fits all?" To which the salesgirl replied, in her thick German accent, "It's a hat. Take it off."

DENISE HUXTABLE/ LISA BONET

The first television character who really had style (and I'm not talking Marcia Brady or Laurie Partridge—I mean a sophisticated New York fashion sense) was Denise Huxtable. And so I tuned in to *The Cosby Show* every week, not for the family-friendly plotlines or Cos's corny jokes, but to see what Denise would wear next. I'm sure Lisa Bonet, who played Denise, had great personal style and had some input. It was all very drapey and Japanese-y and so perfectly '80s. When she got her own spinoff series, *A Different World*, it was even better, since I didn't have to sit through scenes involving her less fashion-inspired siblings, Theo and Rudy, and I could always count on multiple outfit changes for Denise and her best friend, Maggie (played by Marisa Tomei). To this day, there is no one I would rather look like than Lisa.

JANIS

I spent many boring Saturday and Sunday afternoons with my beloved Scavullo books, mesmerized by the before-and-after photos, and reading and rereading the aspirational tales of glamorous women and how they felt about their hair, makeup, and style. A young jewelry designer named Janis was the most captivating woman of all, though. First off, she lived on her own in Manhattan, which right there would have been enough for the sixteen-year-old me. She also had super-long dark hair, beautiful skin, and a striking, ethnic face.

My favorite picture was the one where she had no makeup on at all and was wearing a simple black crewneck (cashmere, I guessed) and a dazzling Art Deco necklace. On the next page, she was dressed in a leopard coat, made up with tons of black eyeliner, dripping in diamonds, and sporting stacks of cool, spiky bracelets. She talked a lot about staying in shape and not wanting to wear what everyone else did. She was twenty-six—which seemed the perfect age to me—and had recently spent a long weekend in London. *Wow.*

Years later, when I was a writer at *Harper's Bazaar*, I nearly fell over when I got to meet her and she gave me a tiny pavé star pendant. I mentioned my favorite photo of her and told her that I had noticed a tiny loop at the end of that Deco necklace and had always wondered if something was supposed to be there. She looked at me like I had two heads and said that she had in fact removed a pendant. I think I freaked her out a little.

✳ It's never too late to reinvent yourself, even if it just means wearing a new kind of shoe or jewelry, or simply cutting your hair.

ANNE H.

As you know by now, my high school was an unfortunate, style-stifling preppy wonderland. Monograms, Bermuda bags, and Fair Isle sweaters were what you had to wear to be popular. I never understood why perfectly cute fifteen- and sixteen-year-old girls wanted to dress like dowdy middle-aged women; they had their whole lives to look like that, I thought. One girl, who had grown up in this look, came back from summer break a changed woman. Her previously long, head-banded hair was in a super-cute, edgy crop, and she'd traded her khakis, add-a-bead necklace, and Docksiders for vintage frocks, 1950s rhinestone jewelry, and pointy-toed flats. Turns out she learned it all in Greece. This look also came via the amazing Belinda Carlisle and the Go-Gos, whom Anne J. and I were obsessed with. While we copied them, we weren't bold enough to really get it right. Maybe a rhinestone earring here, a pointy flat there, and a dab of cheap pink lipstick from Woolworth's, but we were way too chicken to go all the way. When we reached senior year, Anne H.'s look got more hardcore, and she rimmed her eyes with thick black liner and wore pointy black patent-leather thigh-high boots. She crossed a line for me, and what was once fun and different turned into something a little dark.

JANET W.

Janet was one of my sister's friends who had really good style. One outfit I remember was a diaphanous hippie top that had subtle metallic thread running through it, worn underneath a pair of slightly-too-large overalls. Janet was obsessed with David Bowie. She was nice enough to say that, if I agreed (and convinced my sister) that he was not only a great musician but also super handsome, then she would agree that Leif Garrett, my obsession, was hot. Done. Janet later joined a band that played in the East Village (even on school nights!) and got punkier and punkier over time. By graduation, she was wearing full-on thick, dark eyeliner that was flung way beyond the corners of her eyes, a leather biker jacket, skinny black (always ripped) jeans, combat boots, and chains. Rumor had it that she later went crazy after drinking liquid acid, although I'm pretty sure that's not true, since I just saw her on Facebook, riding horses and looking as beautiful as ever.

✳ Let your favorite
music influence
your style, even
just a little bit.

MEG

There was a group of fancy girls one year older than me and my friends who suddenly went from preppy to burnout chic and started hanging in the parking lot with the other real burnouts. Meg was the one who really stood out for me. Most days she showed up at school in her fitted waist-length parka complete with ski tags hanging off the zipper, semi-tacky (and that was really the whole point) lace-up rubber-soled shearling boots, and jeans with a Rolling Stones lips logo patch sewn right on the back of her thigh. I just remember thinking that placement was so clever. Of course I ran out and bought my own patch; I don't recall that I had the nerve to actually sew it on to anything and let her see my bold-faced copycatting, but who knows?

✳ Sometimes one tiny thing can make the difference between boring and unbelievably cool.

ANNABELLA

I definitely wanted to be Belinda Carlisle, Lisa
Bonet, and even Madonna circa her "Borderline"
video, but honestly, no one was ever as cool as
the lead singer of Bow Wow Wow. First of all,
like Lisa Bonet, she was the ideal beauty to me.
Annabella had that perfect skin color and a face
so feminine it could handle even a Mohawk. She
always wore some awesome new-wave African-
print outfit and had tiny hoop earrings tracing
her whole lobe. I imagined her hanging with her
foxy—yet scary—also mohawked guitar-player
bandmate and cavorting all over London with
other funky people doing fun, punky, God-knows-
what British things until all hours of the night.

BROOKE

The first time I ever flew on a plane was in
1982, on the now defunct pay-$19-cash-for-your-
ticket-onboard People's Express, to visit Dana at
Boston University. As I sat in my seat, smoking
cigarettes (when it was still permitted, of course)
in my high school uniform of jeans and one of
my dad's college sweaters, I tried to imagine
what my sister's amazing new life was like. When
I finally arrived on campus, I was immediately
dazzled by all the college girls wearing whatever
they wanted—heels, big Ylang Ylang earrings,
funky leopard-patterned tops, you name it. College was different. You didn't have to fit in, and
it was there that I began to realize how much
cooler it was *not* to.

Back then, there was a Diet Pepsi commercial that featured a boy flirting with a cute girl
wearing jeans and pink pumps, and suddenly
everyone just *had* to look like her, not least of
all Dana. She bought a pair of lipstick-red
high-heel pumps that she wore with tight jeans
or leggings. My first night at B.U., Dana went
to a party and I chose to hang out with a girl
on her floor named Brooke. She wasn't much of

a looker, but Brooke was cool in a different way from Dana—her style was more vintage-y and a little dusty. She had short, boyish red hair and freckles and, unlike anyone else there, wore baggy vintage jodhpurs and old holey sweaters. As soon as I got back home, I found my mom's teenage riding pants, cinched them with an old leather belt, and wore them around the house, vowing that as soon as I got to college, I would be more like Brooke and wear whatever I wanted.

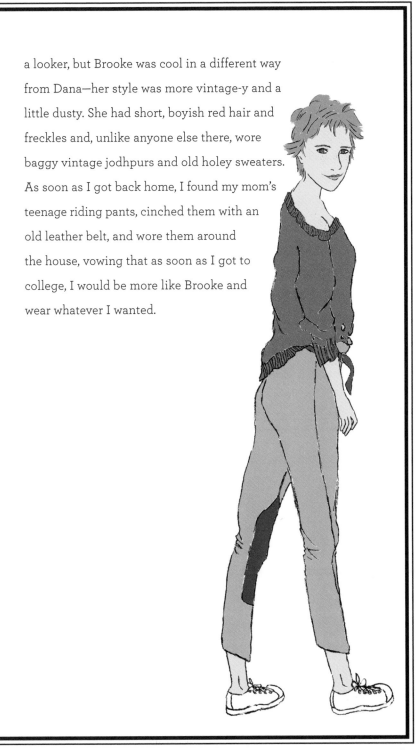

THE HAMPTONS

or

How to Dress As Though
Life's a Party 24-7

favorite
bikini

The summer of 1980 changed
everything. That was the year I
was fourteen and my parents built
a house in the woods by the bay
in East Hampton. Sure, we had
already spent lots of weekends
out there, staying at the Sea Spray
Inn on Main Beach (which sadly
later burned down) or at friends'
houses, but this was a different

and exciting new development—we had our very own house and, hence, the promise of fun-packed, glamour-filled summers. The Hamptons were basically a living dream for me and my friends Kathy and Anne J. This was a place, like New York City, where we could see fascinating people in amazing clothes—tons of models and designers and people with cool jobs at magazines and ad agencies who lived and worked in the city. Aside from fashion magazines and books, this was where we got most of our fashion inspiration. One of our favorite models from *Seventeen*, Marilyn Clark, went to East Hampton High School, and besides, there was a whole slew of new boys who didn't know us yet.

Never mind that no boys ever liked me back home. No one knew me here—I could reinvent myself! I dreamed of meeting a cute boy, preferably a surfer, who would walk me up the long, elevated boardwalk-like path that led to the front door of our edgy new modern wooden house and kiss me under the artsy 1980s structure—with the modern wind chime swaying underneath.

During our first summer in the new house, our mom, who was busy with work, made her father stay with us. Dana and I would hang out on Main Beach all day, while Grandpa Jack, a compulsive gambler, found his own hangout—the OTB in Southampton. Sporting my favorite lavender bikini with purple piping, I would stake my claim in the sand, slathered in some crazy artificial-coconut-smelling SPF-zero oil with the juice of about five lemons in my hair, sipping electric-orange Sunkist (I figured that if drinking it made me look more like the girls in that "Good Vibrations" commercial, count me in). We would lie there for hours and hours reading the new *Seventeens* and *Mademoiselles*, listening to top-forty songs like "Steal Away," "Sailing," and "Rock with You," and talking to local or vacationing boys (we didn't discriminate). Around four o'clock, we'd see Grandpa's giant boat of a car—a dark-green Buick Skylark—in the fifteen-minute parking area. While we loved him to death (he was fun, generous, and a real character), Dana and I would cringe as he would get out of the car looking like a Central Casting mafia hit man—jet-black suit, slicked-back hair, cigar dangling out of his mouth (he never lit them)—hand cupped over his eyes, scanning the beach for us. "We gotta go!" we'd say as we quickly gathered our stuff and ran toward him, hoping no one would ask any questions.

I had already been a semi–mother's helper for one summer (semi because it was for friends and they didn't pay or expect much). But in the summer of '82, Dana and I were hired as real mothers' helpers, for strangers who interviewed us and everything. I made friends with another babysitter named Nina, who I thought was glamorous because her mom was divorced and she lived on the Upper West Side. Nina had a unique shirt made from a flour sack and she taught me how to drink alcohol. We'd hit the town and do what all the kids did: order the dead giveaways, banana daiquiris and piña coladas. I was toying with a preppy/new-wave look back then; I remember a particular pair of soft, loose-fitting button-fly madras shorts that I rolled up at the hem and wore until they were threadbare, with a boy's blue Oxford shirt. I would get a little bolder for nights on the town with Nina or my new local-surfer boyfriend, B.J., like when I bought Crayons to punk up my look. These were sort of like jazz shoes, but not as cool since they were canvas and had clear colored plastic soles (mine were yellow). I went for it anyway because they added a little more height than jazz shoes, which I thought gave me the dreaded small-foot syndrome (when you feel like an elephant in ballet slippers).

Dana and I both got fired from our babysitting jobs on the exact same weekend (me, Nina heard through the grapevine, because I wore skimpy bikinis and spent too much time in my room writing in my diary and smoking cigarettes, therefore making the mother believe all I cared about was meeting boys [Double doy, Mrs. Ditzian], and Dana, because she accidentally slept through her charge screaming for her in the morning). Not wanting to leave what we referred to as "Fantasy Island" (where else could a sixteen-year-old buy a six-pack of Rolling Rock at a gas station as easily as a carton of milk?), we begged our parents to let us stay anyway. Our only hope was the brand-new Häagen-Dazs store that opened on Main Street next to the movie theater. The owner had a bunch of theaters, including East Hampton Cinema, and

work shirt

Bundeswehr tank

favorite club skirt

wrestling booties

thought it was a good idea to open an ice-cream shop right next door, putting his slacker pothead son in charge. We ran into town and applied, each scoring a position. For some reason (peace and quiet?), our parents agreed to the plan and said they'd be back the following weekend with a car. Why they thought it was a good idea to give a couple of boy-crazy teenage girls a car and a house for the summer while they only came out on weekends will never cease to mystify us.

That summer, Dana's best friend, Lisa, stayed with us after a trip to Paris, and we would sit in awe listening to her describe Parisian fashion and hip French words. Back in the pre-Internet days all we had were magazines and firsthand accounts. The biggest coup ever was if you had a friend going to Europe and they could bring you back what you could only get there, like Boy bondage pants from London, or Superga sneakers from Italy. That summer, all the French girls were wearing paper-bag-waist tapered jeans and calling everything "schwett" (cool). That was it—we *had* to have these new French jeans. I can't remember how we got our hands on them, but we did (they must have gotten them in at Bloomingdale's, or my NYC/East Hampton friend Abby may have picked them up on one of her many trips to Europe), and I explained to anyone who would listen that these were what all the French girls wore, *in France.*

When we weren't scooping ice cream and fighting over who got to use the register, or frying ourselves on Main

Beach on our days off, we were counting the hours till we could hit the clubs with our fake IDs. Every night there was something to get excited about—ladies' night, employees' night, you name it, we were (embarrassingly) first in line. I thought a lot about what would look best while I was dancing (if that's what you call skipping in place) to songs like "What I Like About You" and "I Know What Boys Like." This was definitely a time that called for an edgy hairstyle. The manager of Häagen-Dazs was a townie girl with a lot of gay friends and—just my luck—one of them was in beauty school. On my day off, I drove to his mobile home, where he transformed me with an of-the-moment asymmetric bob. I tucked the shorter side behind my ear, just like all the girls in *Mademoiselle*. (This often caused awkward long-hair-sneaking-over-to-the-shorter-side moments; I spent a lot of time pulling those strands back over where they belonged.) And then there was my stellar club outfit: a Bundeswehr tanktop that I only bought after checking with my dad first ("It's just the German army after World War II, not the Nazis," he assured me when I called him at work from a payphone outside Unique Clothing Warehouse), a black cotton tiered mini, black Zodiac wrestling-style boots, and a rubber belt. I nearly burst with pride when a vacationing girl from London complimented my style, until Dana said, "They're not really known for their fashion sense over there. If she were from Paris, that would be another story."

KATHE

That first summer at my parents' new house, I heard some children playing in the neighbors' yard, so I figured I'd go over and offer my babysitting services. "Do you have kids?" I asked the hip man on the deck, who had longish hair and a slight Robbie Robertson vibe. "Yeah, we have kids—what's it to you?" he answered. I was horrified and said I was just wondering if they needed a sitter. He apologized profusely and explained that some other neighbors had complained about noise. He brought me inside to meet his wife. Kathe (pronounced "Kathy") was about thirty and gorgeous, with beachy blond hair and freckles. She was in the kitchen, wearing nothing but underwear and a T-shirt, with a newborn baby in a bassinet on the floor and an adorable, long-haired three-year-old girl by her side. Kathe and her husband, Larry, were the coolest people anyone could ever hope to babysit for. The next year, when I was fifteen, I was their live-in mother's helper and made about thirty dollars a week. They let me smoke, gave me no curfew, and would practically beg me to go out so they could smoke pot and have sex.

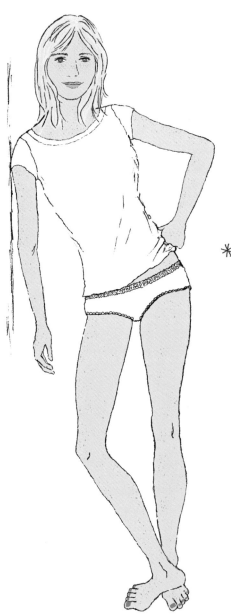

✳ There's nothing sexier than a simple, great-fitting white T-shirt. If you find one you love, buy three!

✳ Be creative with how you wear something to make it your own. If this girl had simply zipped up her jump-suit like the rest of us, she wouldn't have looked as special.

GERMAN EXCHANGE STUDENT

One night, while my friend Anne J. and I waited outside the Windmill Deli for local boys to swing by and take us to a beach party, we spotted the most amazing-looking girl we'd ever seen in person. She had lanky blond hair (which I loved, because mine was thick and brown and at that age, anything's better than what you've got) and wore a mechanic's jumpsuit, unzipped, with the sleeves tied around her waist and nothing but a man's tank undershirt on top. She tucked the pant legs into high-heel leather scrunch boots (even though it was summer). We were all so curious about her, and I asked my older sister if she thought that maybe this girl had kissed one of the boys we liked. She told me I was naïve and that no one her age (sixteen, maybe?) "just kisses."

LAURA

I first noticed her on the beach. She was my surfer boyfriend's first cousin and had crazy-amazing black corkscrew curls and the face of a young Elizabeth Taylor. Laura went to boarding school and drove a BMW 320i, which, she explained, was a starter car for kids her age. She also wore a women's two-tone Rolex with a jubilee band that her parents bought her as a reward for getting into private school. At first I thought the strap was too big for her, until she explained that the cool way to wear a Rolex was loose, with a couple of extra links, so that it spun haphazardly around the wrist. Her aunt was a shoe buyer at Saks, which was why she had a closet full of amazing mid-heels. I bought a baby-blue angora cardigan with little pearl buttons and jodhpur-style pants, thinking it would make me a little more like her. Later, even though Laura was only five foot three, Bruce Weber shot her in some Italian sweater ad and she had a brief modeling career. I recently friended her on Facebook and noticed a couple of weeks later she had mysteriously unfriended me.

MAYA

I saw a lot of interesting people while I was scooping ice
cream in the Hamptons. The model Paulina Porizkova came
in at the height of her career, and so did Joe Elliott from Def
Leppard. I was so awestruck by Paulina (in dark Levi's jeans
and a matching jacket) that I needed confirmation and asked
the guy she was with if she really was my new favorite model.
I heard him tell her and she said, "Yeah, I'm Paulina, what's
it to her?" I was crushed. Then when Joe Elliott came in and
I asked him for his autograph, he was really put out, saying,
"Fine, but you know I'm trying to relax here! I'm on vacation!" The only reason I knew who he was was we had cable,
and therefore MTV, at home in New Jersey. No one in the
Hamptons knew who he was, and I told him so. And anyway
I thought he was a dork for ordering Rum Raisin, the old-
lady flavor, in a cup, no less. It kind of amazed me that two
super-hot celebrities would be so cruel to a sixteen-year-old
fan in a Häagen-Dazs painter's cap and a T-shirt that said
"Boysenberry" on the back, scooping ice cream for minimum
wage. However, there was one amazing girl, Maya, who came
in, with perfect long blond hair, black leggings and flats, and
an Oxford shirt buttoned all the way to the top but with the
collar twisted, so that the right side was attached to the left
button, and vice versa—so incredible. And she was nice to
me! Maya also wore the best lipstick, perfect for her new-wave

sensibility, which she later revealed was Sea Lily Perle by L'Oréal. It was just the perfect opalescent stain, and Anne and I ran out to buy our own tubes. Maya came in to the store a lot and always ordered Swiss Almond Vanilla. She worked the door at Hurrah, one of the hottest Manhattan clubs to move "out east." I gave her free ice cream and she let me and all my friends into the club without IDs.

✳ Trendy doesn't have to mean following to the letter. Maya took the zeitgeist of the new-wave time and made it her own.

✳ Mixing looks is
key. Preppy boys'
pieces like Oxford
shirts calm down
funkier ones like
Hawaiian print
skirts and metallic
shoes.

SIAN

I met Sian on the beach during the summer after I graduated from high school. She was from L.A. and was staying with her mom's ex-husband and his new girlfriend for the summer, which seemed utterly screenplay-worthy to me. She embodied the perfect "preppy punk" mix that I so longed to get right. Sian was way too hip to be hanging out with me; she spent most of her time with surfer boys who also happened to model, and she was one of the first people outside of a magazine that I'd seen wearing Ray-Ban Wayfarers. She also wore Town & Country surf shirts with writing down the sleeves, flippy little Hawaiian print skirts, and pointy electric-blue metallic flats. She took me to her house once and it was the first time I'd ever seen a bottle of Evian, let alone an entire cabinet full—we were strictly a tap-water family; the sophistication made my head spin. She inspired me to buy a Reminiscence Hawaiian skirt of my own, as well as a Town & Country surf shirt that said "This Surf Is Our Turf" on the front (so what if waves scared me?) and a Ralph Lauren Polo boys' blue Oxford shirt. Many post-college years later, at a party in New York, I noticed a girl's feet clad in classic Vans high-tops and thought, "Sian would wear those." I looked up and it was her.

CHRISTA

She worked in a hip clothing store
in Southampton, cut her hair into
a Mia Farrow pixie cut when everyone
else's was long, wore cute '60s-style
sleeveless shift dresses with no jewelry,
and smoked fancy brown cigarettes.
She didn't like me much because I had
once dated her brother and she thought
I was using her to get back to him.
She was kind of right. Which is not to
say I didn't think she was super cool,
anyway.

When you're doing a strong
retro thing, wearing little
or no jewelry somehow makes
the whole look more modern.

COLLEGE

or

I'm Coming Out!

My very first day at Boston University was kind of a bust since my dad made us drive up to the campus later than most people did. This made me the obvious "new girl," so I had to prove myself. Back then my mom smoked a pipe (weird, I know, but before you start picturing a toothless hick puffing on the corncob variety, just know that hers was actually a gift from me—streamlined and chic, complete with mother-of-pearl inlay). So there was Mom, smoking her pretty pipe, and I noticed two girls running around the hall having fun and not bothering to introduce themselves. Finally I yelled "Yo!" which just made them mimic me and run away. My new roommate and I put little notes on all the doors on our floor asking everyone to come by, but that just caused people to make fun of us even more. The hall runners, Holly and Lisa, ended up becoming my best college friends. They later told me they were smoking pot that first day; when questioned by the R.A., they simply said, "Well, that girl's mom was smoking a pipe," and they were free.

I felt like college would be the place where I could finally wear whatever I wanted and feel like I fit in. During orientation, I saw tons of fashion-forward girls from all over the world, most confident in their urban-sophisticated getups. My sister was already a junior and had her look down pat—usually leggings (I remember one pair in a red-and-black zebra print that were actually pajama bottoms) or a miniskirt and colored pumps. I was more into a thrift-store mash-up, like the girls in the bands on MTV wore—like my new favorites, Annabella, from Bow Wow Wow and Downtown Julie Brown, an MTV veejay (with the best job ever, as far as I was concerned).

About halfway into freshman year, I was itching for a change and was still naïve enough to think you could just take a picture of an amazing-looking woman with an awesome haircut to the stylist and come out looking exactly like her. So there I was at the John Dellaria Salon in downtown Boston, holding my Jacques Dessange magazine ad. When I showed the stylist the tear-out of the cute blond with the pouty mouth and kicky short hair, he just nodded and clipped away. I was surprised that I didn't suddenly resemble the model in my inspiration photo; it was still just me, but with short hair.

Then came the never-ending color experimentation—because, hey, when you're young, it's hard to leave well enough alone. Holly and I thought it would be fun to douse our heads in Sun-In, which was basically a spray bottle filled with okay-smelling peroxide. The thing about Sun-In was that you had to be blond for it to work, so our experiment ended up transforming us into a couple of brassy carrot heads, causing everyone to mistake us for one another for the next four years, even when our hair was restored to its natural brown.

Holly didn't care much about fashion—her main thing was that she wanted to look cool (if you told her she looked pretty before heading to a party, she'd bum out and change). But she would go along with almost anything I mandated as long as I convinced her it was cool. I bought a pair of big gypsy chandelier earrings and we each wore one (but someone would invariably ask one of us if we'd lost an earring). Once I decided we should slick our hair back and wear black lipstick (we used eyeliner at first and later found the real thing). The problem was, the stuff we combed through our hair turned out to be curl activator,

Sun In

"Carole Bouquet" earrings

Black lipstick

Dippity Do–style, giving us the completely wrong look. A skater boy that Holly was dating said we looked like JAPs. We were crushed, and she stopped trusting me for a while.

Freshman year was all about oversize army pants, men's blazers with the sleeves rolled up, ripped sweaters, and short, choppy hair, so by the time I was a sophomore, I decided I needed to try to something a little more sophisticated. Someone asked me on a real date (before I had just "hung out" with guys, but this was the first time I was being wined and dined by a veritable stranger!). By then my hair had grown out into a bob and I cut bangs, thinking they would make me look a little French. I wore tight jeans, a simple black long-sleeve T-shirt that slid off the shoulder, and black suede pumps. In my mind we'd be going somewhere like *über*-hip Parisian hangout Café de Flore, but in fact we had dinner in the atrium at the Copley Plaza mall.

The summer I graduated from college, my friend Abby and I went to Danceteria in Southampton on a particularly slow night. A handsome older man asked me to dance, I said sure, and we started talking. This man turned out to be the famed photographer Peter Beard, and when I realized this, I was instantly dazzled. He gave me the code to the gate that led to his amazing property in Montauk, and I would go with my friends and sunbathe on his private cliff as if it were my own.

One day, Peter asked me what I wanted to do with my life. "Not sure; maybe advertising," I said. "You should be a stylist!" he declared. Believe it or not, even though I was a magazine fanatic, I didn't really know what that meant—someone who does hair? He explained it was the person who dresses the model and basically sets up the feeling of the shoot. People actually got *paid* to do that? I was sold.

He decided my first assignment would be a shoot with him and Grace Jones (!!!). He called me on my private teenage line at home in Summit and gave me the heads-up: Grace would be coming on such-and-such a day and I needed to come and style the shots. I made my friend Holly come along, and there we found ourselves—hanging out with Peter, Grace Jones, and Richard Bernstein, the man behind all of those fantastic painted *Interview* covers. I couldn't believe my little college friend and I were actually admitted into this sanctum of unbelievable fabulousness. *So this is what it's like,* I thought. Since it was a hot day in August, everyone was puzzled by our *Dirty Dancing*–inspired rolled-up denim cutoffs and heavy Dr. Martens Oxfords. Peter, who walked around in sarongs and African sandals, was especially curious as to why we were wearing such clunky, orthopedic-looking shoes in the middle of summer. It turned out that Grace had forgotten her makeup and didn't feel like shooting anyway, so we ended up lying on the bed watching her in her James Bond movie while she smoked a joint. And although I never would have lied about it, Peter was nice enough to provide me with copies of the shots he finally took weeks later. "Just say you styled them," he said. "No one will know." I later found out that I actually made it into one of the pages of Peter's famous diary.

Favorite green
sweater

Dirty Dancing Shorts

Doc Martens

JULIE

In college I tried really hard to get that '80s vintage thing down. I had the right pieces, like real army pants, riding boots, and sweaters authentically worn in by me, but somehow I was never able to go all the way and nail it. There were quite a few girls who perfected the look, though, and Julie was one of them—she had grown up in Manhattan and had complete confidence about everything she wore. She had a short, asymmetrical haircut and always strutted around in beat-up paddock boots and big cinched oversize pants. Julie lived on my floor during freshman year, but she didn't invite me over too much because she smoked a lot of pot, and as much as I tried, I never liked it. She was having an affair with one of her high school teachers and would often spend the weekend in New York with him. When they broke up she said, "It's over, but I was a real trouper!"

✳ A cute haircut can
be your signature.

SADE

Even though my best friend, Anne J., and I were in love
with the kooky overstyling that defined much of the
'80s, we were pretty taken with a sultry new singer on the
MTV scene. She was tiny and strikingly beautiful, with
the slightest spattering of freckles, and she always dressed
so perfectly simple—perfect-fitting Levi's (not too tight,
not too loose) along with some kind of bolero jacket and
black cowboy boots. Her hair was usually slicked back, and
she was rarely without giant hoop earrings and matte red
lipstick. Suddenly Sade was the only one we wanted to be.
Anne found a preppy boiled-wool Talbot's jacket in her mom's
closet and somehow made it look very cool and very Sade
one New Year's Eve. She wore it with leather pants, a black
turtleneck, and giant hoop earrings. I didn't have the right
jacket, so I settled for leather pants, cowboy boots, and
big earrings. Sure we only ended up at a restaurant in downtown Summit, New Jersey, but we felt just as glamorous as
if we were our new favorite singer hanging out in London.

MANDY

There were a lot of chic girls doing the new-wave thing at Boston University in the '80s. Some had semi-Mohawks that I knew were made famous by the hairstylist Christiaan (when the hair was down, it just looked like a bob, but when they pulled it back, the shaved sides were revealed—wow). Some wore drapey, Japanesey, druidlike outfits. I also remember two girls with long, curly hair who always hung out together (one had black hair, the other blond—like Betty and Veronica) and who never wore any makeup, save for red lipstick. Their uniform consisted of jeans, a white T-shirt, cowboy boots, and real army dog tags. And then there was Keep-It-Low Lori (so called because when asked what year she was in, she replied, "Freshman—keep it low," even though we were freshman too) who had the perfect monochromatically made-up face. I reported all of this back to Anne in letters to Milan so she could copy accordingly. Sure she was a model with all the tricks at her fingertips, but real-girl college style had its merits too. The one girl who stood out most of all was Mandy. She was super tough and had sexy curly black hair. Her

everyday fall-and-spring going-to-class look was a perfect pair of classic gray sweatpants (I suspect tapered by a tailor), a V-neck white T-shirt, and white gymnast shoes. Her books were thrown into a Louis Vuitton Speedy 40 bag (the biggest one they make), and she flaunted a couple of Bulgari pinky rings that her dad had sent her just to say "hey." She looked great, but she definitely scared us a little. (Of course I tapered my sweats and am now the proud owner of a Speedy 40.)

✳ Mix casual classics like sweats and tees with fancier pieces like a great designer bag.

DEAD-HEAD CLASSMATE

I don't remember her name (Caroline?), but
she was tan, smoked Camels, and always wore
some kind of amazing turquoise or art-nouveau
"lady ring." I loved the bohemian look of her
cigarette pack and the way the brown filter
dangled from her bronzed, ring-clad fingers.
Once in college, I ordered a silver lady ring
from an out-of-the-way biker jeweler in Allston
(you had to go up some ominous musty stairwell to get to his shop). When I finally came
to pick up the finished product, he confessed
that he had accidentally melted it. Then he got
into a fight with another customer and pulled
out a gun. Needless to say, I never got to live
out my lady-ring fantasy.

✳ I still love the look
of the right mix of
silver rings. Try a
big turquoise one
with a couple of
simpler bands.

ESZTER

At some point in college I saw *Stranger Than Paradise*, a super-cool black-and-white indie film about a New York hipster whose teenage cousin comes uninvited to visit from Hungary. At first the guy thinks she's cramping his style, but then they actually become close and go on a trip to Cleveland together. The almost real-time action and plot weren't really what I was so interested in, though. I was more into the young and gritty '80s vibe and the cousin character, Eva, who was played by an actress I'd never heard of named Eszter. She had a thick accent and was even-keeled and blasé, speaking in a monotone voice, rarely reacting to anything. She had choppy bangs and was what the French call *jolie laide* (pretty/ugly). Eva had a real modern beatnik look, mostly wearing black: black turtlenecks; men's black pants; old men's oversize black cardigans; and men's white shirts buttoned to the top, like a modern-day Annie Hall. Eva smoked only Chesterfield cigarettes, a fact that, at the time, I thought was just so funny and amazingly quirky. When I moved into my own studio in 1990, I put a giant *Stranger Than Paradise* poster over my bed and just felt so cool being in the know about such an amazing movie that not many people knew about. Also, it was a pretty great-looking poster. I kind of want another one.

MARTY

In Boston, Holly and I got in with a local skater crowd for a while. We often went to dive bars in "bad" neighborhoods that hosted special hip-hop nights. This was during the height of LL Cool J, the Beastie Boys, and Run-DMC. We were excited by this new scene and bought *Licensed to Ill*—a little after the fact. We didn't want anyone to know this, of course, so we stepped on the tape case and scratched it up so it would look like we'd had it for months. There was one girl who was always around the scene whose style we fell in love with. She was pretty and looked like maybe she had been preppy in high school (having grown up in Summit, I was good at spotting this type) and was now taking chances we wished we were cool enough to take. She had long blond hair that she usually put up in a high chola-style ponytail. Her uniform was a great-fitting T-shirt, baggy Levi's, suede Vans, and giant square gold door-knocker earrings. While I never would have looked as cute in her getup, I did go for the giant hoops years later—just big, round bamboo ones. They've actually become a classic summer staple, and I pull mine out every year.

✳ Buy a bunch of street
gold to wear in the
summer. I love a good
Figaro chain and
big hoops.

THE MAGAZINE YEARS

or

Finding My Real Style

The summer after I graduated from college, I got a part-time job with an exercise-equipment company, offering free trials on lat machines over the phone to gym teachers in high schools. ("May I speak to Coach Kowalski, please?") The rest of my time in Boston was spent with Holly (who actually had a real job as a law intern), sunbathing on her roof, slathered in pure coconut cooking oil. She still refers to that time as the summer I was the color of a penny.

At the end of August, I moved home and started scouring the *New York Times* help-wanted section for jobs. My mom bought me some pumps and lent me a skirt and blazer, and off I went to the city on my job search. One interview was for a position as an assistant at the advertising agency Kirshenbaum Bond (I didn't get it), and I tried a couple of other agencies where a whole lot more of nothing happened. After a few dispiriting weeks, I spotted an ad for editors and writers for a new teen magazine called *Sassy*. Could this be the very magazine I had subscribed to years earlier, which had folded after about three issues? I was obviously not qualified to be a writer or editor or anything close to that level, but I answered the ad anyway and took the bus from Summit to *Sassy*'s Times Square office. There I met with Tina, a super-conservative office manager in a pinstriped skirt suit and a full face of makeup, complete with layered shades of purple eye shadow. Looking back, I'm guessing she couldn't have been more than twenty-six, just a few years older than me, but at the time she seemed really old. She explained that no, this was not the same *Sassy*; this one was in fact based on the popular Australian teen magazine *Dolly* and was headed by a twenty-five-year-old named Jane. Tina let me know about an opening for a receptionist and asked if I would be willing to take a typing test, and even though I only cleared about thirty words a minute, Tina said the job was mine. I was over the moon.

I read the copies of *Dolly* that Tina gave me cover to cover and immediately started trying to dress like the models in the fashion spreads (which were way more progressive than those in American magazines, especially *Seventeen* and *YM*, which suddenly seemed *sooo* uncool). It was all about over-the-knee socks, bubble skirts, and baby-doll dresses, and that's exactly what I started to wear. Every morning, I rode the bus with my dad in to Port Authority (his office was in the Grace Building, down the street from mine) and took the short walk to One Times Square, where I sat at my desk, right by the entrance to the elevator, smoking Marlboro Lights and drinking Diet Coke. In the early days, I greeted all the potential writers and editors on their way in to interview with Jane and became friends with most of them once they were hired. I spent hours gossiping with one of the writers, Christina Kelly, at my desk, often picking up the phone and hanging it right up if we were in the middle of a story—they'd call back, I reasoned. Sometimes the fashion department would ask me if I wanted to get prices and store information for some of the clothes during my lunch break. I was beside myself—I was actually getting on the inside of the secret workings of the magazine machine!

After only six months, I was promoted to fashion/beauty assistant (even though Tina tried to block it), and that's when everything changed. Suddenly, I had the most fun job I could ever have imagined. While my friends were working in corporate offices, wearing gray flannel suits and button-downs, I was in ripped jeans and Doc Martens, going on shoots, traveling, and meeting models and celebrities like Joey Ramone, Liz Phair, and Kim Gordon. After a while I earned the title Fashion/Beauty Editor and was responsible for writing the popular beauty-advice column, "Zits and Stuff," as well as shooting my own fashion stories and covers (even the now iconic one of Kurt Cobain and the then virtually unknown Courtney Love). Soon my father joked, "Who gave you this job? It's like you made it up!"

Sassy was no ordinary prissy teen-girl's magazine. It was hip and funny and real. Now everything is written the way *Sassy* was, but then, it was unheard of. It was a major sign of the times, spanning generations and cliques and becoming a cult favorite of bands like Sonic Youth and Nirvana. Think about it—you'd never see Kurt or Courtney (or Johnny Depp) on the cover of *Seventeen* in a million years. It was such a great place to be that I stayed for seven years, until its last owner, a conservative man who simply didn't know what to do with the magazine, sold it to Peterson, the publisher of *Guns and Ammo* and *Young Miss*. The whole staff was let go, so I quickly reinvented myself as a freelance stylist and writer, working on music videos and step-by-step exercise shoots for fitness magazines and beauty articles—pretty much anything that paid the rent.

In 1996, *Harper's Bazaar* was looking for a fashion writer; a friend of mine knew the fashion features director really well and recommended me. Having only worked at an edgy teen magazine, I was terrified to even call about the job, but I did. They asked me to do a writing test, and I spent an entire weekend in East Hampton writing and rewriting maybe six fashion blurbs, including one on the history of the Birkin bag (which was not as ubiquitous back then), and another on how chunky belted cardigans were great because they were *so* Rhoda Morgenstern. No one was more shocked than I when I was actually called in for a meeting. On the day of my interview, I figured I'd wow them, so I opted for a little-boy's white T-shirt from JCPenney (they fit the best), my go-to Daryl K gray-pinstripe skinny pants, and square-heeled silver vintage sandals, circa 1963. I thought I looked great until I got off the elevator on the seventeenth floor and saw all the girls who worked there, rushing up and down the halls with their perfectly blown-out hair, sleek pencil skirts, and ladylike Manolos. They were the kind of women who actually knew how to use concealer and looked good in every trend. It was like grade school all over again; I just didn't fit in. I'm still scratching my head about this one, but somehow I got the job. This simultaneously elated and terrified me.

Harper's Bazaar was definitely not *Sassy*. Not even close. Back then, no one wore jeans to work, and I actually got in trouble for wearing denim to a fashion show. (It didn't matter that they were my favorite Daryl Ks, *and* I had an agnés b. menswear-style coat over them—I might as well have been

JC Penney
perfect tee

Daryl K. pants

mine

theirs

in Sears Toughskins.) My boss reprimanded me in front of everyone at the show, declaring, "We don't wear combat boots at *Harper's Bazaar!*" I was actually wearing cute red wedges—albeit vintage—but she saw what she wanted to see. (What about all the chicly disheveled French editors across the runway?)

Another time, our very cool editor in chief, Liz Tilberis, asked me if my fur sweater was Dries Van Noten. "No," I replied, feeling proud of my distinctive fashion sense and assuming she would too. "It's vintage!" The boss was there to witness the interaction; she was horrified and said I should have just lied and said it was Dries. I didn't get it. I mean, really—wasn't it cooler to have personal style and not only rely on designers? Somehow, though, I made it through, and even though I wasn't exactly raking in the dough, I ended up loving the job and everything that went with it—covering fashion shows in New York, Milan, and Paris, and editing big features.

Then in 1999, my friend Kim called me to ask if I would leave *Bazaar* and help her on a top-secret magazine project for Condé Nast. The only thing was, she couldn't tell me any details, and asked if I would please just leave my job and come do this. Even though the beloved Liz Tilberis had recently died after a long battle with ovarian cancer and I knew a new editor was bound to come in and clean house, I just couldn't make a move without all the facts. When she finally told me it was a magazine about shopping, even though the project was only to create a prototype, I left skid marks on the light-gray carpet on my way out of *Bazaar.*

The funny thing about *Lucky* (which at the time had yet to be named—*Mine* was under consideration until we realized it was kind of obnoxious) was that back then you had to be a certain kind of girl to work at Condé Nast. And let's just say neither Kim nor I was that kind. Kim was a hip entertainment journalist specializing in rock stars, and it was pretty much a freak accident that I was at *Bazaar*. We never dressed up, never wore the latest runway trends, and never hung out with the fashion crowd. Neither one of us owned a pair of fancy shoes or an "it" bag (although when I took the job at *Lucky* I commemorated it by buying a Marc Jacobs Venetia bag in Caramel). Sure, I was crazy about fashion, but in a different way. While I liked what was on the runway, my favorite part about going to fashion shows was seeing all the European editors filing in with their fabulous outfits, awe-inspiring jewelry, and wonderfully messy hair.

The head of human resources at Condé Nast was definitely not happy about having me join her empire. I wore jeans and beat-up boots every day and had long, unruly hair. Horrors! When she actually had the gall to rag on Grace Coddington's "awful hair," I knew I was at least in good company and took her disdain for me as a compliment. Somehow, Kim and I slipped through the cracks; we were excited about making a magazine for women who loved clothes and style, but didn't want to be preached to by a bunch of snobs. At first, people scoffed at the idea of *Lucky*, but it turned out to be the most successful start-up in Condé Nast history.

Vintage fur sweater

First big purchase

Second big purchase

JANE

The editor in chief of *Sassy* was named Jane.
She was young to have that job (about twenty-
five) and was often in poufy miniskirts with
knee-length leggings under them and cute
nerdy glasses. She also wore the same pair of
scuffed regulation police officer shoes every
day for years. I was thrilled that I hadn't gotten a job at a corporate ad agency (where I'd
previously been interviewing) and instead
had ended up here, wearing cute clothes like
Jane did every day.

✳ If something
works, make it
your uniform.
You'll save hours
in the morning!

✳ Wear what you love.
Mix classic designer
pieces with edgier
ones for an interesting
hodgepodge look.

MARY

When *Sassy* was just staffing up, a really cute woman came in to interview for the beauty editor position. She was teeny, with long, dark, wavy hair and short French-girl bangs. She was wearing a chic black mini-kilt and ankle boots, and soon she got the job. (Mary was the godsend who finally rescued me from the HR maven, Tina, by hiring me as the fashion/beauty assistant.) In the beginning, she wore little Comme des Garçons pleated miniskirts and asymmetrical jackets, and often had a bandana artfully wrapped around her head. Later, she moved on to oversize overalls and clogs. Now she wears stacks of Hermès Chien bracelets and Chanel pendants. And she loves a good hat. Whatever her look is, Mary always has something fun and funky going on.

✳ Don't be afraid to take chances just because no one else is wearing something. If you like it, go for it.

JACINTA

Jacinta was one of my bosses and the fashion director of *Sassy* magazine. She came all the way from Sydney, where she had been the fashion director of *Dolly*, the Australian magazine that *Sassy* was based on. For a few years her look was very rock-and-roll, complete with a head bandana, Satan ring, and Cult T-shirt. After that she went through a classic phase and cut her long hair into a bob.

On a trip to Paris with her Australian boyfriend, she bought a simple, Hermès Bolide–like bag that I didn't understand at the time, but I figured she knew what she was doing. My favorite look of hers was around the time she fell in love and got engaged to an American guy and she offset her ultra-traditional solitaire ring with a micro cut-off denim miniskirt and Ugg boots. (This was a few years before anyone in the States even knew what Ugg boots were.)

JANET M.

When she first started at *Sassy*, covering the market and calling in all the clothes for our shoots, I thought she might be too genteel and I couldn't figure her out. So everyone teased in a sing-song, "Andrea doesn't like the new girl . . . " Janet was from Maine and I just saw her for what she seemed to be—a tall and skinny athletic girl who lacked the *Sassy* edge. I was *so* wrong. She turned out to be neurotic and hilarious (qualities which often go hand in hand) and lots of fun.

Once we went to Miami together for a swimsuit trade show and stayed at the Century Hotel. In the mornings, I would sit and have my breakfast while Janet went for her daily run. Then she'd plop down, light a cigarette, and we'd start our day (which seemed to consist of walking in unbelievable heat and smoking even more Marlboro Lights). My favorite outfit of Janet's was a scoop-neck, short-sleeve black leotard with a tiered knee-length ethnic skirt of black cotton. She wore this with a wide beaded African cuff that she'd bought on a backpacking trip through Africa, along with a black stretch headband and an agnès b. Lolita backpack (which she wore on her trek up Kilimanjaro, earning the nickname "Lolita" from the locals).

✳ You don't need to
change your style for
every activity.

CHRISTINE

One of the most fun things about working at *Sassy* was going on shoots—that was where you could really feel all the glamour and the magic. Even if you were just shooting some tiny photo that would run in a front-of-book column instead of a big glossy spread, at least you weren't stuck at a desk, and you were almost always listening to good music and joking around on set. I met Christine, a makeup artist, on one of these shoots and immediately became obsessed with her style. She was tiny, had long blond hair, and was the perfect mix of classic, rock-and-roll, and biker chic. She wore a boy-size stainless Rolex, and her uniform was always skinny flat-front trousers and a fitted button-down. Her husband rode motorcycles and she decided to get her own—a sexy little Moto Guzzi that she would ride to her shoots, wearing a tiny Bellstaff jacket (I am here to say that she was truly the first girl ever to wear one—in New York, anyway). Later she became a designer and opened a store on Crosby Street in SoHo, which quickly became the go-to place for hip downtown girls. She now owns the best store in the Hamptons and basically wears a new variation of the same perfect uniform she did twenty years ago.

✳ When you have
  a closet full of
  classics, you
  can wear them
  forever.

✳ What worked for you in your teens won't necessarily work as you get older. Allow yourself more understatement and a little more glamour as you age.

CHLÖE

Jane, the editor in chief of *Sassy*, became really well known, landed her own TV talk show, and hired me to be her personal stylist. While working on a commercial for *The Jane Pratt Show* around Sixth Avenue and West Fourth Street, I spotted a girl at a newsstand wearing giant beige corduroy overalls and a handmade turbanlike patchwork hat. She told me her name was Chlöe, that she was from Darien, Connecticut, and that she was cutting school for the day. I begged the producers to put her in the commercial. They were confused by her appearance, seeing her as weird rather than stylish, but they finally agreed, and afterward she and I swapped numbers so she could model for *Sassy*. Chlöe's mom ended up calling to say that modeling was fine, but could her daughter also be our intern? We said, "Sure." Now she's a famous actress and fashion icon whose style has evolved into something more chic and glamorous.

JENNIFER

She worked at agnès b. back in the late 1980s, when all the sophisticated, artsy people shopped there. My friend Anne J. and I studied how she wore her little printed skirts and snug-fitting T-shirts with black clogs. We were really into her not only because we loved how she dressed, but also because she looked like Anne's older sister, Mary, and they both looked like the singer Patty Smyth when she was in the band Scandal. We all tried to dress like Jennifer—super simple, but with a subliminal rock-and-roll edge.

My dream back then was to have a whole wardrobe filled with agnès b. My mom took me shopping there for my birthday once and I got a black silk blouse. (I was going to look like Bob Dylan!) In those days I also wore my must-have agnés b. snap cardigan into the ground. Then when the teenage line Lolita came out, we all wore T-shirts and backpacks with the cute script logo on it. Jennifer also had a silver rolling ring from Tiffany and a delicate sparkly antique diamond band that was her grandmother's, which Anne J. and I still refer to all the time as the perfect ring.

KATE M.

While I was working at *Sassy*, I bought an issue of the UK
style bible *The Face*, which featured the most amazing (and
now iconic) black-and-white image on the cover. Though the
girl in the photo was very pretty, she didn't look like any
of the models I was used to seeing. She was all goofy smiles,
with no makeup, and her hair was stringy and of a neither-
here-nor-there shade. And that outfit! She was wearing
a kids' Native American headdress and what seemed to be
a triangle-top bikini with only a skinny strap visible. The
accompanying images inside were just as casual, with styling
that looked like the model had dressed
herself. These seemed more like
snap-shots of a cute girl on
vacation taken by a
friend than a profes-
sional endeavor. The
clothes were simple and
wearable—little agnès b.
skirts, tank tops, and rubber
flip-flops. It was all so easy and
understated and real. I was instantly
smitten with the stylist, Melanie Ward
(who I later worked with at *Bazaar*), and
the photographer, Corinne Day. I begged

my boss, Mary, to call in this model for a go-see. When she finally came in (I was beyond excited to see her in person), she was wearing chunky-heeled, knee-high vintage boots and was carrying a leopard handbag that I'd often spotted in her off-duty pictures. Of course, she became ultra-famous a minute after that and we never got to use her.

✳ When in doubt, Google "Kate Moss." You can never go wrong with a "WWKD" tactic.

DARYL

In 1991, a little boutique called Daryl K opened up on East Sixth Street and it changed my life (style-wise, at least). This was long before good, affordable fashion was everywhere, and cool stuff was still hard to come by. The boutique felt really raw and punk, like something you might find in London (although I hadn't been there yet). The racks were lined with the most incredible hip-hugging, boot-cut skinny pants anyone had ever seen. This was suddenly the only place to shop if you wanted to be edgy. The owner/designer's name was Daryl. She had an awesome Dublin accent and was the epitome of rock-and-roll chic, more like a lead singer than a designer. I bought her pants in almost every fabric—denim, black upholstery velvet, white vinyl, and leather (the last of which Daryl custom-made for me herself!).

Too much of one look is never a good idea. Daryl balances her rock-and-roll style with classic gold or modernist silver jewelry.

SHARON

I met Sharon when she was a salesgirl at
Daryl K. She was edgy but cute, with black
hair and skinny knee-length Daryl K pants.
She always had on some kind of interesting
vintage shoes that had nothing to do with cur-
rent trends. She didn't need anyone to tell her
how to dress; she just wore what she liked. She
was a painter from Ohio, and I decided that
I needed her to assist me right on the spot.
Now she's a stylist; she still paints and makes
amazing one-offs, like reconstructed T-shirts
and crazy chiffon scarves.

BROOKE W.

I was styling a music video and the director had his friends
(including me) make cameo appearances. Brooke was a
super-cool friend of the director; she co-wrote a couple of
soungs and did vocals on the Beastie Boys' *Hello Nasty*
album—that's her on "Picture This." In this video, she played
herself (a fashion photographer) and wore a hot purple
A.P.C. blouse, pointy Beatle boots, and black patent-leather
pants that made her ridiculously long legs look even longer. And that hair . . . so perfectly big and wild. She wore
her friend Jill Platner's handmade silver jewelry; the rings
looked particularly fetching on her long, elegant fingers. I've
bought some myself, hoping I would look like Brooke—no
dice, sadly, although I do love every piece of Jill's jewelry.

✳ Make classics like cashmere cardigans and skinny jeans instantly chicer by loading on strong, ethnic jewelry.

LESLIE

Anne J. and I were obsessed with French *Glamour*. I loved looking at what was going on in Paris, the city I most longed to visit. There was one story in the November 1989 issue that we completely flipped over. It featured our favorite model, Leslie Navajas, running through industrial-looking streets, smoking cigarettes and wearing skinny leather pants, pointy boots, cashmere sweat-ers, and loads of silver Turkoman jewelry. We spent years trying to perfect this look—classic with a bohemian edge—and even bought expensive silver-and-carnelian Turkoman cuffs at the old Craft Caravan store on Greene Street in SoHo. We were always (and actually still are) in search of the perfect dangling chandelier earrings, which we refer to as Carole Bouquet earrings, since we once saw a picture of the French actress/model in a pair.

ELISSA

There was one person at *Bazaar* who always looked amazing by never following trends or overdoing it. No one did minimalism like Elissa. She was a fashion-sittings editor, and was wickedly funny. Her spreads were always my favorites, whether it was Kate Moss in a little skirt and pointy pumps, or fashion stories that were all about accessories. For Elissa, less was more. She always wore simple, well-made pieces, like knee-length A-line skirts and crew-neck cashmere sweaters, without ever looking boring—maybe it was her cool angular face and messy-ish hair, or just her attitude in general. The only adornment she ever wore was her wedding band and a skinny gold Katharine Hamnett tank watch.

✳ She once told me you should never wear your engagement ring with your wedding band; "It looks like a housewife set," she said. I remembered that when I got married.

* Sometimes a fur (even fake) just makes a crappy day feel more glamorous.

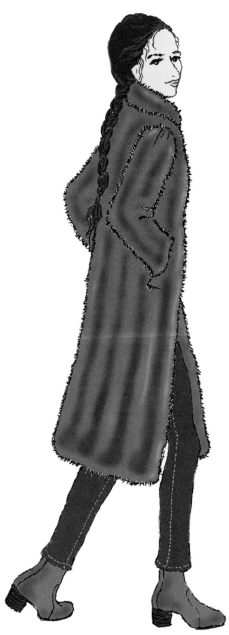

STRANGER IN A FUR COAT

I was walking down Newtown Lane in East
Hampton one winter afternoon when I scoped
a woman I now wish I'd taken a picture of. She
was wearing a midi-length old-school lady's
mink coat, jeans, and beautifully nondescript
stack-heeled leather boots. Her only acces-
sory was a long, sleek braid. I imagined that
her rich mother had handed that coat down
to her. She was very ballerina-in-the-'70s à la
Turning Point. She wasn't trying to be anything, she just was. I think of her every single
winter when I've had it up to here with my
giant parka.

CHRISTIANE

When Calypso St. Barth first opened in 1995, it caused a real style revolution. Finally, there was something new and sexy and colorful that made a whole bunch of buttoned-up city girls suddenly want to look like they lived on the beach in St. Barts. Calypso sold an eclectic look and the promise of a bohemian lifestyle like the one lived by its creator, a French woman named Christiane. She had the looks of a model and the style of a chic beach bum—loose caftans, mixed colors, and ankle bracelets. And when I saw the fierce tattoo of a Native American chief just above her ankle, I knew she had an edge, and possibly a wild history.

＊ If it works at
the beach, try
it in the city.

ALYSSA

Alyssa and I worked together for a bit in different departments at *Harper's Bazaar* (she was in bookings), but we didn't really become friends until I started traveling to L.A. a lot for *Lucky*. She was small, with the perfect brown skin tone (her mom is Brazilian) and artistic, expressive hands. She wore the best thrift-store dresses and always anchored them with big shit-kicker boots or '70s clogs (also vintage). She worked at the Whiskey Bar at the Sunset Marquis for a while and was forced to wear a cheesy, very un-her black catsuit. But she made it her own by adding Gene Simmons–style black platform boots and she was suddenly her fabulous self again.

LORI

Lori owns one of the most famous tattoo shops in New York, as well as an everything-you-could-possibly-want urban emporium called Love, Adorned. When we first met, she completely intimidated me with her hip looks and unflappable demeanor. She's got tattoos all over her body—even her hands—but on her, it's elegant . . . . Maybe it's because she has the face of a 1930s movie star (Lori loves a good hat and is the only person I know who can get away with wearing a cloche). She's never without her Affenpinscher dog, Birdy, who can sometimes be mistaken for a furry clutch (which comes in handy when she wants to sneak her beloved pet into restaurants). Thanks to Lori, I'm still contemplating finger tattoos.

✳ Know yourself and create the right harmony. Lori balances her tattoos with beautiful hats and jewelry and feminine dresses.

KATE C.

Kate had a chipped front tooth and reminded
me of Jodie Foster in the 1970s. She made cus-
tom leather pieces and mostly wore her own
designs. One time she came into my friend
Lori's tattoo shop wearing the most insane
fringed suede poncho, and she looked
just as relaxed and confident as someone
in a classic peacoat. Even though I wished
I could pull off an outfit like that,
or, better yet, one of her suede
halters, I chickened out and
bought one of her braided
leather bracelets instead.
I loved listening to Kate
talk about how they
were "trick braids." I've
looked that up a few
times, but I still can't
figure out how she made them.

It only takes one crazy piece
to make a big impression.

✳ Reinvent yourself
slightly every
couple of years to
keep things fresh.

MAUD

On a *Lucky* photo shoot in Paris, we booked local hair and makeup artists to save money. It's always a plus when someone shows up who not only is talented but also serves as the day's fashion inspiration. Maud was really petite and gorgeous, with cocoa-colored skin. Her outfit sent me into an I-didn't-pack-right-for-this-trip frenzy. She showed up in a belted hand-blocked cotton Indian dress, white lace tights, and black patent-leather ankle-strap Mary Janes. I was riveted. I couldn't wait to book her again! She has since moved to New York, where I'm lucky enough to run into her from time to time. She goes between rock-and-roll and much more classic—jeans, tees, Hermès bag, some layered gold pendants—and I *still* want to be her. My husband recently spotted her on her bicycle and the first thing I asked was, "What was she wearing?" Naturally, he hadn't noticed.

OLDER WOMAN ON SHELL BEACH

During our honeymoon on St. Barts, my husband and I were lying on the beach when an older couple (maybe in their mid-seventies) ran into the surf. The woman had on a tiny bikini bottom and no top. Her hair was long, gorgeously wavy, and full-on gray. She was a cross between a Victoria's Secret model, Georgia O'Keeffe, and photographer Harry Callahan's wife and muse, Eleanor. On the beach, this woman, probably French, was so sexy and romantic that I vowed never to give in to those women-over-a-certain-age edicts of having to wear a one-piece bathing suit or chop off your hair.

✳ Who says women have
  to change their style as
  they age?

BLOND TATTOOED STRANGER

My friend Lori and I came across a regal-looking, probably European woman browsing around a store in East Hampton. She had her yellow hair in a simple ponytail and wore a crisp white button-down shirt. What was so remarkable about her made both Lori and me do a double take: On each side of her face, right by each ear, was a tiny tattoo of a green snake. Our thoughts started racing—was this woman a former LSD-dropping Marrakesh hippie? Did she used to hang out with Jim Morrison? Was she covering face-lift scars? We were floored. And although I am confident that I will never in a million years want tattoos on my face, there was something about her individuality that inspired me.

WOMAN AT ST. MAARTEN AIRPORT

On the way back from a trip to St. Barts, my husband and I had a stopover at the St. Maarten airport. In the sea of couples and families in shorts ordering beers and hoagies, I spotted a woman who reminded me of a younger, more refined Yoko Ono in classic clothes. Her hair was almost waist-length and a little frizzy (in a good way) and she had pulled it into a simple ponytail, the rest covered by a Panama hat. Her jeans were dark and straight. I can still see her eating a small bag of potato chips with her white blazer over her shoulders . . . I wish I owned her simple black almost-briefcase-style Prada bag.

✳ If you have one amazing
feature, like super-long
hair, it makes classic
pieces look chic and edgy,
never dowdy.

AFTERWORD

Now that I've settled into a look that's become "me"—some iteration of skinny or flared jeans, good T-shirts or a button down, with maybe a hippie top thrown in; a nicely cut jacket of some kind and dresses for special occasions and hot weather only; and a scarf, always a scarf, even in summer—I don't feel compelled to copy everyone I see. Still, that doesn't stop me from getting excited and inspired by random people every day and appropriating a teeny part of their look. Almost every day, I stop in my tracks and think, "Wow, she really knows what she's doing," while I'm walking to work, sitting in a restaurant, or shopping around, and I want to thank all of those women in advance for inspiring me.

I would also like to thank the following people, who believed in *I Want to Be Her!* from the get-go and who are a big part of everything I do: my oldest friend, Anne Johnston Albert, because I can't draw to save my life, and because, aside from being a big fan of her work, no other illustrator could ever capture so perfectly what lives in my memory; my cool parents, Caryl and Gene Linett (his amazing style inspires me as much as my mom's), who introduced me to cool movies and music and all things good and encouraged my love of style and fashion from a very young age; Dana Linett-Silber, my big sister, who always showed me what was what; my niece, Libby Silber, who inspires me every time I see her; Uzi Silber; Asher Silber; Oona and Louise Albert, such chic, smart kids, and their dad, Martin Albert, for putting up with this project; my other "sister," Hollis Salzman; Lisa Pandelly Nagar for giving me so many great sartorial memories; David Rees and Ron Anderson, my own rooting section, who always make me feel like I'm doing the right thing; Daniel Howell for encouraging me in everything I do and for making me laugh like no one else can; Kim France, a supportive friend and collaborator for so many years; Christina Kelly, with whom I tried many a look while we lived together during our *Sassy* days; my awesome agent, Jason Allen Ashlock, who was excited about this book when others didn't get it; Mitch Zamarin for introducing me to Jason; my patient and encouraging editors Rebecca Kaplan and David Cashion; Ethan Hauser, who proofreads the blog, just to be nice; my other parents, John and Irene Waring; Liz Kiernan, (such a g'buk!); Madelyne Bailey; and of course, my husband, Michael Waring, who is truly a mensch and the best creative partner anyone could ask for, and who continues to shoot our blog (even when he'd rather be out on some motorcycle adventure), and who always girl-watches with me and points out the best ones wherever we go.